Living
the art of
Loving
a picture book

Living
the art of
Loving

a picture book

written and illustrated by
Lara Match

New City Press
Hyde Park, New York

Published by New City Press
202 Comforter Blvd.,
Hyde Park, NY 12538
www.newcitypress.com

Living the art of Loving
A picture book

Cover design and layout by Lara Match

Library of Congress Control Number: 2022943980

ISBN: 978-1-56548-543-3 (Paperback)
ISBN: 978-1-56548-544-0 (E-book)

Printed in the United States of America

Contents

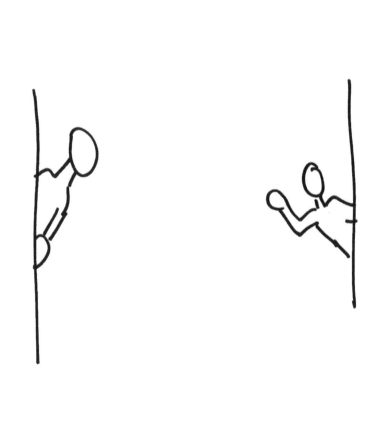

Introduction

Sometimes we walk into a gathering full of apprehension and, as we feared, almost nothing goes right. Other times, we are enjoying a connected moment with someone and suddenly we're in the middle of a fight with them. We can't recall what happened, how to rewind or if we even want to. Sometimes, we get to a certain time of year and remember a person who is important to us, but with whom we no longer speak.

We are all so fragile. A look, a gesture, a pause can fray the weave between us all and similarly can thread us back together. For how many dinners have we been absent or distracted? How many conflicts have we been unable to face? How many times have we wanted to be understood, but felt no one noticed us?

This is a book about living the art of loving, a set of practices that help me and others to reset—often, dozens of times a day—with more love and more openness than we had in the moment before. When I live the art of loving, I feel rooted and in control, ready for, expecting even, surprise and conflict.

When you turn the page, you'll see an illustration on the right side and some minimal text on the left side. This layout continues throughout the book. Each picture shows a single moment within a common interaction, and the scenes unfold almost like a flip book.

The first scene is two people, both absorbed in their own thoughts, when one of them decides to make room for the other, and they establish a connection.

The second scene follows the same pair as they build on the bond from before, but then lose it unexpectedly. This time, both of them make space for one another in order to renew their harmony.

The third scene begins with two connected people entering a gathering where it would be easy to become reactive. But they decide to stay rooted to their purpose of loving each other and the people around them.

The fourth sequence shows a larger number of people as they prepare to welcome a newcomer, aiming to provide an environment that is both safe and honest.

The fifth interaction begins with an offense which distorts the individuals, making it harder to seek and to find the good in each other.

The final sequence is deeply personal and follows the internal passage of someone into a dark place from which they acknowledge their situation and yet still choose to rise and love.

The last few pages briefly outline the history of a global movement born out of World War II, from which the set of relationship techniques called "The Art of Loving" were developed.

Living the art of loving feels courageous, it feels generous, it feels smart and it feels–good. It has the capacity to breathe life into relationships that have been abandoned, to begin to resolve issues with coworkers or partners, and to answer so many awkward moments when we have asked ourselves "What do I do now?".

Please enjoy this dynamic little book that can be read in ten minutes cover to cover if you like to read fast, or at a more reflective pace. I encourage you to try reading this aloud with some friends or family, each person reading a page around a circle and then trying out the discussion questions at the back. For me, this has led to some of the best conversations I've had in years.

This is a hopeful little book. It relishes the great gift we are to each other. It conveys a sense of agency and urgency to our relationships. I hope the drawings on these pages touch your heart. I hope the words you read here feel real. I hope we all discover what can only be learned when there is mutual love. I am excited for you to turn the page!

In unity,
Lara

What is unity?

We all have thoughts.

It takes a moment to even notice
that another person is there.

To make room for them,
we let go of our thoughts.

This is not easy to do.
It takes time and focus.

With effort, we clear our minds and spirits,
freeing the space to welcome the other.

We become an empty container for them.

So empty that we almost don't exist.

They sense our openness
and begin to speak.

Our emptiness draws them out,
like a vacuum.

There is a momentum to their sharing, as
the stumbling blocks have been removed.

We become immersed in their ideas,
feeling them as our own.

This generates mutual respect
and mutual care.

In the other person,
we find ourselves.

The good in them
is like the good in us.

We arrive at a state of
connectedness and harmony.

Here, the ideas feel new.

There is a clarity that seems
beyond either of us.

Some people call this unity.

How do we keep unity with each other?

Unity makes us feel comfortable,
capable, and creative.

Solutions reveal themselves
more easily.

Together, even normal tasks
seem magnificent.

And, just like that, unity can break.

We don't always know why
the connection is lost.

Sometimes it's ego, apathy, or a flaw
we noticed in the other person.

Someone has to be the first
to start again.

We both let go of our thoughts and make room for each other.

We are open to the good in them.

And they are open to the good in us.

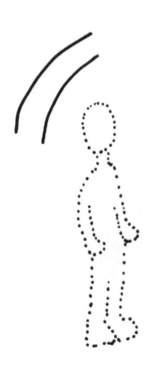

Into the space we've each made, the best
parts of ourselves are drawn forward.

Our ideas flow with ease
and are received with gentleness.

We are separate but feel close.

Again, we arrive at that state of connectedness and harmony.

Here the ideas feel new and there is a clarity that seems beyond either of us.

Each day, we build, break, and repair unity.

To keep unity, we are as committed to repairing it as to building it.

How do we build unity
in a new place?

Sometimes, we are the
newcomers to a gathering.

Before entering, we remind each other
to let go of our thoughts, making space
for those we may meet inside.

We lift away our nervousness, our prejudice, and our desire to be liked.

We even let go of the unity between just the two of us, and its beauty, ready to build something new and inclusive.

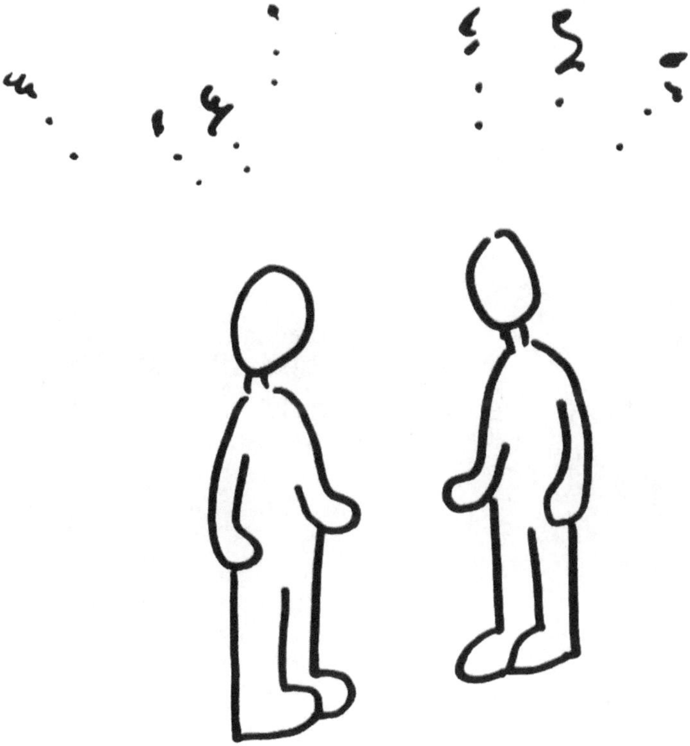

We arrive open and interested,
able to see and affirm the good in others.

We do not need to be side by side
to build unity in this new place.

While we may not know precisely how to
stand or what to say, finding something loving
to do makes us feel capable and creative.

We attend to the unique needs of each
person, checking that no one is left out.

We participate in the activities that the others enjoy, trying to match their pace and their mood.

Our attention has a quality that is both unwavering and relaxed.

It inspires those nearby to be more thoughtful listeners too.

The atmosphere in the room settles as it becomes clear that we hold each other in high esteem, even if some of our opinions differ.

The intensity of genuine care is almost startling at first.

An idealism surfaces as we each gain access to the part of us that is selfless.

Mutual love forms a base, and unity surrounds us, like a gift. We feel clearheaded and purposeful.

We are aware that this time is precious and we want to protect its unique beauty, built with this exact set of people.

How do we invite
others into our unity?

Before a newcomer arrives, we often come together to prepare.

We ready the space and prepare our hearts, making room for the guest.

A group of people has many
thoughts to loosen.

We set them aside and devote
ourselves to openness.

The guest takes priority and we talk
about what is happening in their lives.

Maybe one of us knows them best,
and we tell the others something
about their pursuits and interests.

We begin to enter their world
even before we greet them.

The newcomer arrives,
carrying their hopes and burdens.

Because of our preparation,
they experience an immediate sense of safety.

When the whole room is in tune,
the guest can be honest.

Sadness is shared, heard, and held.
Joy is shared, heard, and held.
Connections are illuminated and
ways forward become visible.

There is a mood of excitement and discovery.

We learn something about ourselves
just by being in this atmosphere
of care and attention.

On occasion, we agree ahead of time to be
mirrors for each other, reflecting back the
strengths, and maybe weaknesses we observe.

We offer our feedback with great care and
a pure desire to see the other succeed.

It is well-received when trust is
present in the relationship, and
trust is present in that moment.

Moments of truth are a delicate but powerful
way to help each other grow and improve.

What do we do with conflict?

We never seem prepared for hurt.

Something tightens and there isn't room
for us anymore. The change is swift.

It is often unclear if the others
notice we no longer feel safe.

We trip over another offense
and our hearts race.

Looking up, the others have become distorted.

We see only their negative attributes.

We are incredulous.

Maybe we should leave.

They seem to place no importance
on the values we live by.

They appear unattractive,
unrefined, undisciplined.

We feel righteous and deserving.

Maybe we should stay.

Sometimes it is us feeling
misunderstood or misheard.

Sometimes we are the ones making
mistakes, and others give up on us.

We do not know their hearts, their
intentions or their trials.

The window to heal is narrowing.

Time is slipping and interest is moving away.

Whatever we do feels risky.

Something they say or do will probably hurt us again. It is likely that we will hurt them too.

But, if we do not accept this risk of hurt, we will not listen long enough to understand.

We brace ourselves and loosen our grip on the fear.

With humility and courage, we return.

We reconnect to the part of us
that is generous and patient.

The more we are open to the good
in each other, the more good we
all seem able to produce.

We learn the words that have different meanings to each of us, and find the precise places where our thinking begins to diverge.

Even when we don't agree, there is a peace in understanding where each person is.

We share enthusiasm for the goals we are able to work toward together, and withhold some of our disappointment when we are not able to share more.

Our full selves are rarely known by one party, but aspects of us are seen and honored in each of the groups where we participate.

What do we do with suffering?

We all have something
we're really sad about.

Sometimes, when we are alone, our hidden hurts rise up, looming large and close.

We feel defensive, angry, embarrassed.

We are vulnerable.

A rush of vivid imagery compels us to revisit many troubling memories at once.

We sink with the weight of an irreversible change, real or imagined.

Everything seems dark, insurmountable, and in disarray.

The sting echoes loud, then quiet,
in time becoming still.

Our sadness is near and pressing,
but distinct from ourselves.

Why!

For a moment, we feel suspended,
as though the pain is held back, and
we enter an unsteady calm.

We were abandoned by someone we rely on.

We failed to achieve what we had hoped.

We are confused about how to proceed.

We wonder what we could have done
differently, knowing what we know now.

A part of us wants to move
forward, but we can't yet.

Sadness grips us in a self-satisfying lull
that doesn't want to be disturbed.

Time slows and begins to feel unproductive.

With effort, we make our decision.

The past is untouchable, the
future, unknowable. The present
moment waits to be claimed.

The first step toward others
can be very small.

We go and find someone else.

Everyone around us has needs,
and we offer to help.

Doing an act of love cracks us open.

Regaining awareness of those around
us makes our problems seem smaller.

We all experience suffering, but not at the
same time. One receives good news when the
other hears bad, and the other way around.

So we take turns, ready to set our pain aside
and join in regular tasks with others, while
looking for the right time, with those we trust,
to ask them to enter our suffering with us.

Together we determine how to love
through the difficulties we face.

Many of the ideas in this book
came from Chiara Lubich, founder
of the Focolare Movement.

About the Focolare

Chiara Lubich (Kee-AR-ah LOO-bick) was a charismatic leader (1920-2008), who began her work in 1943, during the Second World War.

While taking cover in bomb shelters, Chiara asked what was worth living for that wouldn't crumble. Inspired by her Catholic faith and together with a few friends, she began to love the people in her war-torn city of Trent, Italy, sharing food and clothing and giving hope.

Chiara and her young community were given the nickname, "Focolare" (Foh-koh-LAR-eh), which means "hearth" in Italian, because of the warmth and family feeling they exemplified.

The small community grew into the worldwide Focolare Movement, which emphasizes unity between people in concrete and practical ways, with love as a radical force for good.

Chiara received recognition for her peace efforts, including the Templeton Prize for Progress in Religion (London, 1977), the UNESCO Prize for Peace Education (Paris, 1996) and the Human Rights Award of the Council of Europe (Strasbourg, 1998), as well as numerous honorary doctorates from universities around the world.

The Focolare Movement operates projects like model villages, where everyone in residence lives the art of loving, and offers fresh approaches to education, politics and business.

A word from the Focolare's founder

We must "make ourselves one" with every neighbor perfectly, by cutting away everything that stands in the way.

Many factors can deter this.

Sometimes we are distracted. At other times we have a desire to rush in with our own ideas or give advice at the wrong time. Sometimes we are poorly disposed to "make ourselves one" with our neighbors because we feel they do not appreciate our love. Or we may be hindered by our negative judgments about them. We might even be harboring an unconscious desire to win them over to our cause.

Sometimes we are incapable of "making ourselves one" because our heart is already preoccupied with its own problems, concerns and agendas.

How then can we "make ourselves one" and let the preoccupations, sorrows and anxieties of our neighbor find a way into our heart?

It is absolutely necessary to remove and eliminate everything that fills our mind and heart. Yes, we have to "cut away" in order to be more open, more disposed to love. We must "do some pruning" in order to love better.

Chiara

Chiara Lubich
The Art of Loving
New City Press, 2010

Discussion questions

So...

- Do you have a favorite image in this book?
- What did it make you think of?
- Which image creates the most struggle within you?

Well...

- Was there a time recently when you were able to be the first to love or the first to start again?
- Do you remember a time when you were able to see the good in someone, even when it was hard?
- Can you recall a time recently when you felt loved and listened to?

And...

- What is one thing you think will stick with you from reading this book, something you'll think of again after you put it down?
- Is there someone you want to share this book with?
- For tips on how to share a book like this or to host a book discussion, visit livingtheartofloving.com.

Thank you

Merle and Molly Mullins - for showing.
Grace (Graziela) Goes - for teaching.
Katie (Mullins) Novak - for believing.
Father Paul Shuda - for affirming.
Ezra Match - for seeing.
Hortensia Lopez - for assuring.
Emma Daley - for laughing.
Tayyaba Bhatti - for knowing.
Jamie Rosenberg - for steadying.
Rabbi Ron Muroff - for listening.
Peter and Sara Lee - for accepting.
Philomena Sheridan - for welcoming.
John Castañon - for explaining.
Renata Dias - for encouraging.
Janna and Craig Match - for asking.
Lara and Kris Novak - for celebrating.
Ellie Friedman - for hoping.
Gary Brandl - for continuing.
Ronen Match - for playing.
You - for reading.

About the author and illustrator

Lara Match is a thoughtful artist, mother, gardener and optometrist. She, along with her four siblings, was taught the art of loving from a young age. Like all families, they experience challenges—different faith practices, different political opinions, different parenting styles—but putting the art of loving into practice has helped them remain a close-knit extended family as adults.

Lara is happy to share these techniques in plain language and with simple illustrations for those seeking close and authentic relationships. She lives in Harrisburg, Pennsylvania, with her husband, Ezra, and young son, Ronen. They would love to have you over for tea sometime.